The Atlas of
Famous Battles
of the American
Revolution™

# The Battle of Trenton

## Wendy Vierow

The Rosen Publishing Group's
PowerKids Press™
New York

*To my dad, an expert on Washington's crossing*

Published in 2003 by The Rosen Publishing Group, Inc.
29 East 21st Street, New York, NY 10010

First Edition

Editor: Nancy MacDonell Smith

Book Design: Michael J. Caroleo

Photo Credits: Cover, title page, pp. 15 (map), 16 (map), 19 (map) Maria Melendez; cover, title page (background map), pp. 4 (map), 7 (map), 8 (map), 20 (map) Map Division, Library of Congress; cover, title page, pp.4 (Howe), 8 (bottom), 12 (bottom) © Bettmann/CORBIS; cover, title page, p. 12 (Sullivan) Emmett Collection; pp. 8 (top and bottom left), 16 (bottom left), 19 (top right) Print Collection, Miriam and Ira D. Wallach Division of Art, Prints, and Photographs, New York Public Library, Astor, Lenox, and Tilden Foundations; pp. 4 (bottom left), 12 (inset left) © CORBIS; p. 7 (inset) © SuperStock, Inc.; pp. 7 (bottom), 11 (insets), 12 (inset right), 20 (bottom) Dover Pictorial Archive Series; pp. 8 (inset), 15 (bottom), 16 (inset), 19 (bottom and inset) © Culver Pictures; pp. 11 (map), 12 (map) Nick Sciacca; pp. 11 (bayonet), 15 (gun) courtesy George C. Neumann Collection, Valley Forge National Historical Park, photos by Cindy Reiman; p.16 (bottom) © North Wind Picture Archives.

Vierow, Wendy.
The Battle of Trenton / Wendy Vierow.— 1st ed.
    p. cm. — (The atlas of famous battles of the American Revolution)
Summary: Provides an overview of the Revolutionary War battle that took place at colonial Trenton.
Includes bibliographical references and index.
  ISBN 0-8239-6333-0 (lib. bdg.)
1. Trenton, Battle of, 1776—Juvenile literature. [1. Trenton, Battle of, 1776. 2. United States—History—Revolution, 1775–1783—Campaigns.] I. Title. II. Series.
  E241.T7 V54 2003
  973.3'32—dc21
                                                                            2002000160

Manufactured in the United States of America

# Contents

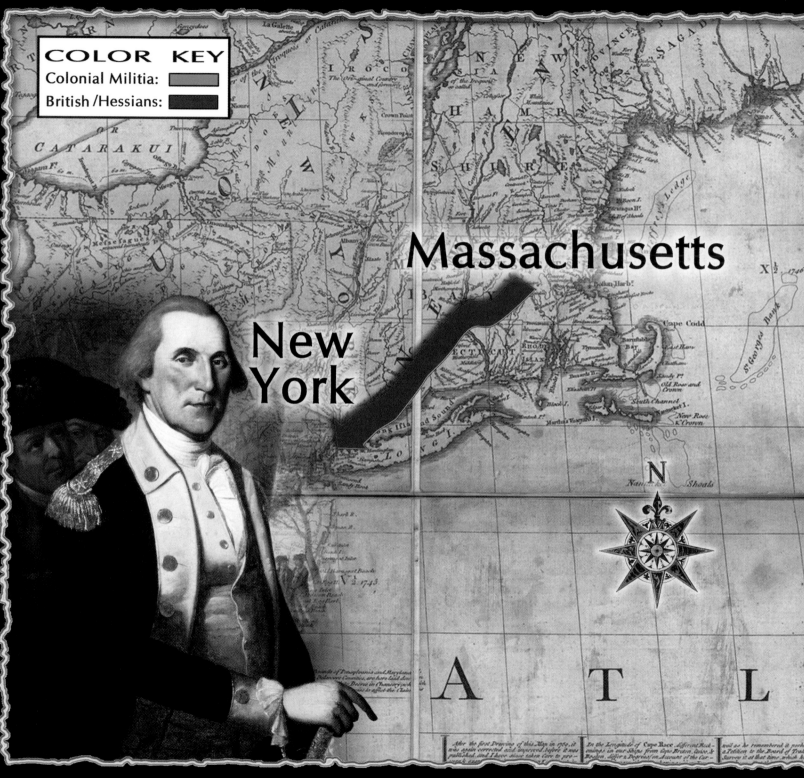

COLOR KEY
Colonial Militia:
British /Hessians:

Massachusetts

New York

N

ATL

▲

*General William Howe*

▶

*Continental army soldiers can be seen in the background of this portrait of General George Washington.*

# Americans Fight the British

The Battle of Trenton took place fewer than six months after the United States declared its independence from Great Britain on July 4, 1776. The **American Revolution**, which started in April 1775, began in the colony of Massachusetts. After losing many battles to the Americans in Massachusetts, the British decided to fight in New York. They thought that by winning battles in New York, they would be able to cut off the New England colonies from the rest of the colonies. In this way the British hoped to win the war. The British army won many battles against the **Continental army** in New York. American general George Washington was commander in chief of the Continental army. He was a skilled soldier, farmer, businessman, and politician from Virginia. In New York, Washington often fought against the army of British general William Howe. Howe was the second commander in chief to take charge of the British forces since the war began. The previous commander was replaced because he had failed to defeat the Americans.

*New York was important because of its location between New England, where the Revolution began, and the other colonies. The British hoped to end the Revolution by capturing New York.*

# American Troops Leave New York

After losing many battles in New York, Washington and his army **retreated** from New York into New Jersey in November 1776. British major general Charles Cornwallis and his troops followed Washington. Washington and his army escaped the British by crossing the Delaware River into Pennsylvania. Instead of following Washington across the Delaware River, General Howe ordered General Cornwallis and his troops into winter **quarters** in New Jersey towns, including Trenton and Princeton. It was the **custom** for European soldiers to stop fighting in the cold and stormy weather of winter and to wait for better weather before continuing to fight. Washington did not plan to stop fighting. He knew that by the end of December, many of his soldiers' **enlistments** would be up. His soldiers enlisted, or joined, the army only for a certain amount of time. Washington needed to win a battle so that soldiers would rejoin the army to fight more battles.

*The Continental army crossed the lower Delaware River from New Jersey to Pennsylvania to get away from the advancing British.* **Bottom:** *General Washington ordered his troops to destroy any boats on the Delaware River so that the British could not cross the river and follow them.*

to
New York

Delaware
River

Princeton

Maidenhead

Trenton

N

**SCALE**
0 1 2 3
miles

**COLOR KEY**
Colonial Militia:
British Regulars:

*Major General
Charles Cornwallis*

One in three soldiers fighting for the British were Hessian.

Soldiers in the Continental army wore many different types of uniforms.

←Trenton

## COLOR KEY
Colonial Militia:
British /Hessians:

## SCALE
0   1   2
miles

Delaware River

N

# Washington Crosses the Delaware

General Washington decided to attack Trenton, New Jersey, which was controlled by British and **Hessian** troops. Just after sunset on December 25, 1776, Washington and his troops began to cross the icy Delaware River. They crossed the river in small, sturdy boats that could carry horses and cannons as well as soldiers. A winter storm was raging. Although Washington wanted to attack Trenton before daybreak, the storm delayed his army. They did not get across until about 3:00 A.M. They were not ready to march to Trenton until about 4:00 A.M.

Washington hoped that no one would see his army and that his attack on Trenton would be a surprise. However, a **loyalist** from Pennsylvania wrote a note to Hessian colonel Johann Gottlieb Rall stating that Washington's army had crossed the Delaware River and was marching to Trenton. Rall put the note in his pocket. Rall never read the note to find out that Washington and his army were on the way.

*The Continental army crossed the Delaware River 9 miles (14.5 km) north of Trenton.*
**Inset:** *Colonel Rall was playing cards and relaxing that Christmas night.* **Bottom:** *General Washington and his troops had no protection from the wind, snow, sleet, and hail.*

# American Soldiers March to Trenton

General Washington asked his troops to be quiet and to march in the dark so that they could surprise the Hessians. The snow and sleet from the storm made the soldiers' guns wet. If the gunpowder became wet, the guns would not fire. Washington ordered the men to attach **bayonets** to their guns. If the soldiers' guns would not fire, the army would use their bayonets to fight the Hessians. Washington was determined to take Trenton on December 26, 1776.

Luckily for the Americans, the Hessians had decided not to send out an early morning patrol, as was their custom, to look for enemies. The patrol was cancelled because of the storm.

The storm also helped to hide the Americans as they marched toward Trenton. Some reports say that two men froze to death during the 9-mile (14.5-km) journey to Trenton.

*After landing in New Jersey, the Americans marched inland to Trenton. **Top Inset:** After the cold, wet crossing, the troops had to march to Trenton in the snow. Some of the men had holes in their shoes and many men did not have winter coats. **Bottom Inset:** The cannons also had to be taken to Trenton. In this image, General Washington directs the movement of the men and the cannons.*

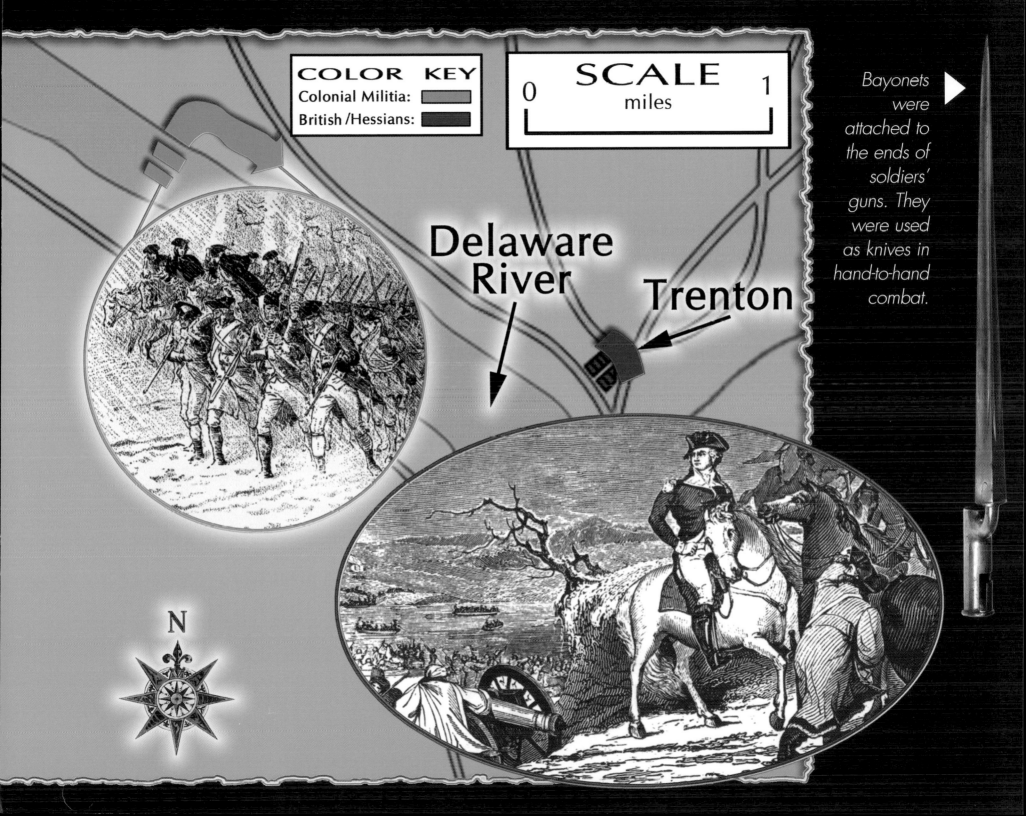

**COLOR KEY**
Colonial Militia:
British /Hessians:

**SCALE**
0    miles    1

Bayonets
were
attached to
the ends of
soldiers'
guns. They
were used
as knives in
hand-to-hand
combat.

Delaware
River

Trenton

N

Nathanael Greene was one of the youngest generals in the Continental army.

SCALE

0 .5
miles

COLOR KEY

Colonial Militia:
British /Hessians:

N

Delaware
River

Trenton

▶

General
John
Sullivan
was a
lawyer from
New
Hampshire.

# American Troops Surprise the Hessians

Major General Nathanael Greene and Major General John Sullivan were marching with General Washington to Trenton that snowy morning. Both men served under General Washington in the Continental army. Washington planned to attack the Hessians by dividing his army among his generals. Washington and Greene would enter Trenton from the north. Sullivan would enter Trenton from the south.

Greene and Sullivan arrived at Trenton at about 8:00 A.M. on December 26, 1776. As planned, Greene marched into the northern part of the town, and Sullivan marched into the southern part of the town. The Hessians were taken by surprise. They did not expect the Americans to attack in a storm or so soon after Christmas. The Hessians had to wake up Colonel Rall, who was still sleeping after a night of Christmas celebrations. Rall quickly mounted his horse and gathered his troops.

*By splitting up, the Continental army was able to attack Trenton from the north and the south at the same time.* **Top Inset:** *General Washington gave the order for the army to split up.*
**Bottom:** *The Hessians were not ready for battle when the Americans attacked Trenton.*

# The Americans Surround the Hessians

Although their guns were wet and were not working well, the American **artillery** did work on December 26, 1776. American soldiers entered houses in Trenton to dry their guns. Soon they were shooting at the Hessians from the safety of buildings.

General Greene's and General Sullivan's troops moved into position to surround the town. Although Hessian soldiers tried to break through the American line, they could not. The Americans continued to fire on the Hessians with guns and artillery. When some Hessians abandoned their artillery because of American fire, the Americans quickly captured their artillery.

Some Hessian and British soldiers escaped over Assunpink Bridge. Sullivan led American troops to the bridge, which crossed Assunpink Creek in Trenton. The Americans guarded the bridge to cut off any more escape attempts. The Hessian and British soldiers were now trapped.

*The Continental army quickly surrounded Trenton.* **Inset:** *The Americans used the abandoned Hessian cannons as well as their own.* **Bottom:** *Soldiers were posted at the Assunpink Bridge to keep Hessian and British soldiers from escaping.*

This rifle was used by an American soldier during the Revolution.

Assunpink Creek

Assunpink Bridge

## COLOR KEY
Colonial Militia:
British /Hessians:

N

Apple Orchard ←

Assunpink Bridge →

King Street ←

Queen Street

*This is a Hessian soldier from the time of the American Revolution.*

N

COLOR KEY
Colonial Militia:
British /Hessians:

# The Hessians Try to Escape

The Hessians tried one last attack on the Americans on December 26, 1776. They marched north toward King and Queen Streets. The Hessians were a perfect target for the Americans, who shot at them from houses and alleys. This type of fighting was not in the European **tradition**. In European wars, armies lined up and shot at each other. The Hessian attack on the Americans failed.

Colonel Rall sent a group of Hessians to see if escape was possible over Assunpink Bridge. However, the Americans controlled the bridge. American soldiers also blocked any escape to the south. Rall ordered his troops to reassemble in an apple orchard southeast of town. Soon after giving the order he was wounded. He later died from the wounds. Other Hessian officers decided to attempt an escape toward the orchard. However, they soon found that Americans blocked the way.

*The Hessians first tried a European-style attack near King and Queen Streets. When that failed, they tried to escape over Assunpink Bridge. Other Hessians headed for the apple orchard to see if they could escape that way.* **Inset:** *Groups of soldiers would fire their guns at the same time. Their guns didn't work very well, so this gave them a better chance of hitting what they were aiming for.* **Bottom:** *The dying Colonel Rall is shown looking ill and giving up his sword, a sign of defeat.*

# The Hessians Give Up the Fight

The Hessians who tried to escape through the apple orchards **surrendered** to the Americans on December 26, 1776. Other Hessians who tried to escape over Assunpink Bridge were forced to surrender.

Some Hessians decided to cross Assunpink Creek in order to escape. Those who crossed the creek found American soldiers waiting for them on the other side and surrendered. The battle of Trenton was finished. The Americans won the battle in less than two hours.

More than 400 British and Hessian soldiers did manage to escape during the battle, but the Americans still took about 900 prisoners. One hundred and six Hessians had been killed or wounded. The Americans also took possession of the Hessians' supplies, including guns and wagons. The wounded Americans totaled only four. Some accounts say that no Americans died. Others say that two were killed in battle.

*American troops captured Hessian and British soldiers at Assunpink Bridge. General Washington convinced most of his soldiers to rejoin the army because of the American success at Trenton.* **Bottom:** *When they realized the Americans had overpowered them, many Hessians tried to escape. Most were taken prisoner.*

Assunpink
Creek

Assunpink
Bridge

N

COLOR KEY
Colonial Militia:
British /Hessians:

Officers
in the
Continental
army often
chose to
wear
blue
uniforms
with red
facing.

The Hessians were
forced to surrender
and become prisoners.

against THE KING'S TROOPS IN NEW JERSEY
from the 26th of December, 1776 to the 3d of January 1777.

Six Miles

**COLOR KEY**
Colonial Militia:
British /Hessians:

# Princeton

# Trenton

*These are two different uniforms worn by American troops at the time of the American Revolution.*

N E W   J E R S E Y

Pennington

Maidenhead

Allenstown

Kingstown

LOSS at TRENT
December 26th 1776
Regt. of Anspach or L
1 Lt. Colonel, 1 Major, 1 Captain, 3 I
38 Serjeants, 6 Drummers, 9 Musicia
206 Rank and File.

Regt. of Rall.
1 Colonel, 1 Lt. Colonel, 1 Major, 1 Capta
2 Surgeons Mates, 25 Serjeants, 8 Dr
officers Servants, 244 Rank and File.

Regt. of Knyphause
1 Major, 2 Captains 2 Lieutenants, 2 I
Drummers, 6 Officers Servants, 258 Ra

Regt. of Artillery
1 Lieutenant, 1 Sergeant, 1 officer's Serv
Total _ 1 Colonel, 2 Lt. Colonels, 3 Ma
12 Ensigns 2 Surgeons, 92 Serjeants,
25 officers Servants, 740 Rank & Fi
6 double fortified brass 3 Pounders w
3 Ammunition Waggons
12 Drums
4 Colours
betwixt 20 & 30 Killed

# The British March to Trenton

General Washington's soldiers were happy to have won the Battle of Trenton on December 26, 1776, but they were also tired. Even though the battle was over, the winter storm was not. At 12:00 P.M., Washington and his troops began to march in the snow and sleet back to Pennsylvania with their Hessian prisoners. By the next morning, the army had crossed the Delaware River. Many American soldiers had been awake for more than 36 hours.

Americans celebrated General Washington's success at Trenton. Washington became a hero, despite the fact that he had lost many battles in New York. Americans who had given up hope of winning independence changed their minds. Many now thought that they had a good chance of winning. Soldiers in the Continental army were also encouraged by the success at Trenton. Almost all of them rejoined the army.

*General Washington and his troops marched from Trenton to Princeton, a distance of about 10 miles (16 km), in the middle of the night.* **Bottom:** *General Washington was able to continue fighting because almost all of his men had signed up for another six weeks.*

# Americans Gain Hope

With the reenlistment of most of his soldiers, Washington was able to continue the fight against the British. On December 30, 1776, the Continental army returned to Trenton and waited for **reinforcements**. Meanwhile, British general Cornwallis moved from Princeton, New Jersey, toward Trenton with about 8,000 men. On January 2, 1777, Cornwallis reached Trenton. He planned to attack the next day. However, American troops slipped by Cornwallis's army during the night. The next morning the Continental army attacked the British at Princeton. The Battle of Princeton was another **victory** for the Continental army.

The Battle of Trenton was an early American success in the Revolution. It gave Americans hope. The war would continue until September 1783, when Americans would finally win their independence from Great Britain.

# Glossary

**American Revolution** (uh-MER-uh-ken reh-vuh-LOO-shun)  Battles that soldiers from the American colonies fought against Britain for freedom from 1775 to 1783.

**artillery** (ar-TIH-luhr-ee)  Cannons, or other weapons for firing missiles such as cannonballs.

**bayonets** (BAY-oh-nets)  Knives attached to the front ends of rifles.

**Continental army** (kon-tin-EN-tul AR-mee)  The army of patriots created in 1775 with George Washington as commander in chief.

**custom** (KUS-tum)  The accepted, respected way of doing something.

**enlistments** (en-LIST-ments)  Amounts of time for which soldiers join the armed forces.

**Hessian** (HEH-shen)  A German soldier who was paid to fight for the British during the American Revolution.

**loyalist** (LOY-uh-list) A person who is loyal to a certain political party, government, or ruler.

**quarters** (KWOR-turz)  A place to live or stay.

**reinforcements** (ree-in-FORS-mehnts)  Extra troops sent to strengthen another group of troops.

**retreated** (ree-TREET-ed)  Backed away from a fight.

**surrendered** (suh-REN-durd)  Gave up a fight or battle.

**tradition** (truh-DIH-shun)  A way of doing something that is passed down.

**victory** (VIK-teh-ree)  The winning of a battle or contest.

# Index

# Primary Sources

**Cover, Page 12 (Bottom Left).** *General John Sullivan.* Engraving, artist unknown, date unknown. Print Collection, Miriam and Ira D. Wallach Division of Art, Prints, and Photographs, New York Public Library, Astor, Lenox, and Tilden Foundations. In this portrait, General Sullivan wears several pieces of clothing that are signs of his military rank. One is an epaulet, a stiff, triangular piece of cloth with fringe on the end that is attached to his left shoulder. Sullivan wears a gorget, a half-moon shaped piece of metal, on a ribbon around his neck. The gorget was all that was left of the armor that knights once wore in battle. Sullivan also wears a red silk sash around his waist. A sash could also be used to carry a man if he was hurt in battle. Only officers could wear signs such as epaulets, gorgets, and sashes. The Continental army could not afford uniforms for all its soldiers, so these signs were very important. They were sometimes the only way to know who was in charge. **Page 8 (Bottom).** *George Washington Crossing the Delaware.* Oil on canvas, Emmanuel Gottlieb Leutze, 1851. The Metropolitan Museum of Art. This is one of the most famous paintings about the American Revolution. It was painted by a German artist who had spent time in the United States as a child and made many return trips there as an adult. Leutze wanted to show the importance of this event in American history, so he changed some details to make the painting more dramatic. For example, the crossing took place in the middle of the night but Leutze showed the sun rising to symbolize that General Washington was leading his troops to freedom. Leutze painted the men carrying the first Stars and Stripes, a symbol of the fight for independence. In real life, this flag was not made until six months after the Battle of Trenton. Leutze also showed future president James Monroe helping a soldier hold the flag. Monroe fought at the Battle of Trenton but he did not cross the Delaware River in the same boat as General Washington. **Page 8 (Top Right), Page 16 (Bottom Left).** *Hessian Soldiers.* Watercolor on paper, Friedrich Konstantin von Germann, c. 1777–1782. Print Collection, Miriam and Ira D. Wallach Division of Art, Prints, and Photographs, New York Public Library, Astor, Lenox, and Tilden Foundations. Von Germann was a soldier under Colonel Rall's command as well as an artist. During the time he was in the colonies fighting for the British, he made drawings of his fellow soldiers. The soldier pictured on page 16 was named John Ulrich Zeth. Zeth joined the Hessian army in 1776, at the age of 17. After the Revolution, Zeth stayed in the United States and married an American woman named Honour Burgoon. They settled in Maryland and later moved to Pennsylvania. Zeth's descendants still live in Pennsylvania. **Page 11 (Right).** *English Long-Land Pattern Bayonet.* Steel, c. 1770s. George C. Neumann Collection, Valley Forge National Historic Park. American soldiers were trained to use bayonets by European officers. Bayonets were very important in eighteenth-century warfare. Once a soldier fired his gun, he had to rely on the bayonet attached to the end of his gun to protect himself. The bayonet was used like a knife to stab enemy soldiers. This type of bayonet was shaped like a triangle. It made a more serious wound than did a bayonet with a straight blade.

# Web Sites

Due to the changing nature of Internet links, PowerKids Press has developed an online list of Web sites related to the subject of this book. This site is updated regularly. Please use this link to access the list: www.powerkidslinks.com/afbar/trenton/